What you didn't Learn

BIODUN **S**AMUEL **A**DEPETU

All rights reserved

What you didn't Learn

COPYRIGHT © 2015

BIODUN SAMUEL ADEPETU

No Part of this book may be reproduced, stored in a retrieval system or transmitted in any form or by any means, electronic, mechanical, including photocopying, recording, scanning, or otherwise, except as permitted under Sections 107 and 108 of the 1976 US Copyright Act, without either prior written permission of the publisher, or authorization through payment of the appropriate per-copy fee to the Copyright Clearance Centre, 222 Rosewood Drive, Danvers, MA 01923, (978) 750-8400, (978) 646-8600. Requests to the publisher for permission should be addressed to: sammydaniels3@yahoo.com, +234-803 826 1705; 809 558 0812

Unless otherwise stated, all spiritual quotations are from the Authorized King James Version of the Bible.

Limit of Liability/Disclaimer of Warranty:

The publisher and the author make no representations or warranties with respect to the accuracy or completeness of the content of this work and specifically disclaim all warranties, including without limitation warranties of fitness for a particular purpose.

No warranty may be created or extended by sales or promotional materials. The advise or strategies contained herein may not be suitable for every situation. This work is sold with the understanding that the publisher is not engaged in rendering legal, accounting, or other professional services. If professional assistance is required, the services of a competent professional person should be sought.

Neither the author nor the publisher shall be liable for damages arising here-from.

The fact that an individual, organisation, or website is referred to in this document as a citation and/or a potential source of further information does not imply that the author or publisher endorses the information that the individual, organisation, or website may provide or recommendations it may make. Further, readers should be aware that internet websites listed in this work may have changed or disappeared between when this work was written and when it is read.

"Stay away from people who belittle your ambitions, small people always do that, but the really great ones make you feel that you too can become great" – Mark Twain

PREFACE

It is often said that nothing teaches better than experience - yours or those of others. However, it is better, more sensible, and safer to learn from other people's experience, rather than from yours!

In Africa, it is often said:

"Esin iwaju ni t'eyin nwo sa're".

You learn from the successes and pitfalls of those before you.

One of my former directors, at a tourism and hospitality services outfit, used to tell us back then that it's better to learn from your predecessors' experience because they've been through the grind-mill before you, and they know the optimal way of getting things done with minimal personal or joint cost.

While I've tried to outline lessons I learnt on the job

through this book, please note that the lessons itemised are based on personal opinion and perception of events in the work environment of the different organisations where I've had the privilege of working.

Given the above, it is just fair that I let you know that the opinions and suggestions expressed are not strait-jacket rules!

And... I'm not empowered to enforce compliance and adoption of these suggestions.

Please feel free to adapt those you may not be able to adopt all the way, to suit the circumstances peculiar to your own work environment.

Thank you for buying this book.

B.S.A.

June   **2015**.

TABLE OF CONTENTS

INTRODUCTION

LESSON #1: YOU NEED PRAYERS FOR INSPIRATION

LESSON #2: ALWAYS PUT ON YOUR THINKING CAP

LESSON #3: FIND OUT ABOUT PROSPECTIVE EMPLOYERS

LESSON #4: BE READY TO LEARN AND ADAPT TO THE COMPANY STRUCTURE

LESSON #5: PUT IN THE HOURS

LESSON #6: FALL IN LINE: LEARN AND ADOPT THE CULTURE

LESSON #7: KNOW YOUR COMPANY'S KEY FINANCIALS

LESSON #8: IDENTIFY MENTORS AND LEARN FROM THEM

LESSON #9: LEARN TO SUPERVISE YOURSELF

LESSON #10: BE CAUTIOUS ABOUT DISCUSSING POLITICAL ISSUES

LESSON #11: PUT UP YOUR GUARDS AND BE ON TOP OF YOUR GAME

LESSON #12: CORPORATE POLITICS IS REAL: LEARN TO PLAY THE GAME

LESSON #13: RESPECT PEOPLE ACROSS BOARD

LESSON #14: UPDATE YOUR KNOWLEDGE ABOUT YOUR NEW EMPLOYERS

LESSON #15: DO WHAT YOU'RE TOLD

LESSON #16: FIND AND OPERATE WITHIN YOUR LEVEL

LESSON #17: AVOID BEING A NUISANCE

LESSON #18: DON'T BE A TOXIC STAFF

LESSON #19: KEEP IT OFFICIAL

LESSON #20: IMPROVE AND POSITION YOURSELF FOR PROMOTION

LESSON #21: STAY AWAY FROM INTIMATE RELATIONSHIPS

LESSON #22: HUMILITY IS KEY

LESSON #23: THINK INDEPENDENLY, EMPATHISE AND COMMUNICATE OBJECTIVELY

LESSON #24: INTRODUCE YOUR IDEAS WITH CAUTION

LESSON #25: DON'T PLAY "I TOO KNOW" (ITK)

LESSON #26: BE PUNCTUAL

LESSON #27: MAKE AN IMPACT

LESSON #28: PATIENCE PAYS MULTIPLE DIVIDENDS

LESSON #29: DON'T START WHAT YOU CAN'T SUSTAIN

LESSON #30: GEAR YOURSELF UP TO SOLVE PROBLEMS

LESSON #31: PRACTISE THE THREE F's

LESSON #32: CONSULT: YOU DON'T KNOW IT ALL

LESSON #33: YOU NEED EMOTIONAL INTELLIGENCE

LESSON #34: EXPLOIT GREEN-HORN OPPORTUNITIES

LESSON #35: LEAVE YOUR BAGGAGE AT THE GATE

LESSON #36: RESPECT THE OATH OF CONFIDENTIALITY

LESSON #37: AVOID EYE-SERVICE

LESSON #38: WORK SMART: OPTIMIZE YOUR TIME ENERGY AND MATERIAL RESOURCES

LESSON #39: PUT YOUR TALENTS TO USE

LESSON #40: THINK BEYOND YOUR PRESENT EMPLOYER

LESSON #41: CHANGE WHAT YOU CAN

LESSON #42: BE A CHAMPION OF YOUR TEAM

LESSON #43: BE ON THE SIDE OF INTEGRITY

LESSON #44: DON'T PUT YOUR COLEAGUES DOWN

LESSON #45: DON'T LOOK DOWN ON ANYONE

LESSON #46: MANAGE INTER-PERSONAL RELATIONSHIPS

LESSON #47: EFFECTIVE COMMUNICATION IS IMPORTANT

LESSON #48: LEARN TO SMILE

LESSON #49: DESIRE TO SUCCEED AND PURSUE EXCELLENCE

LESSON #50: PURSUE A DISCIPLINED HEALTH REGIME

LESSON #51: DON'T CHEAT YOUR EMPLOYERS

LESSON #52: DON'T ALLOW YOURSELF TO BE CHEATED

LESSON #53: DRESS APPROPRIATELY

LESSON #54: LIVE WITHIN YOUR INCOME

LESSON #55: MANAGE YOUR CONQUESTS

LESSON #56: MAKE YOUR EXIT IN AN ACCEPTABLE MANNER

LESSON #57: APPRECIATE GOD ALWAYS

INTRODUCTION

The corporate environment, though a non-militarised zone, is constantly in a cold-war mode with unwritten rules and codes of engagement.

Strategies and tactics adopted are, more often, an off-shoot of those of conventional military warfare:

Intrigue, deception, provocation, manipulation, disorientation, demoralization, deprivation, debasing, arm-twisting, mis-information, grudge-and-revenge, opportunism, direct attack, surprise attack, flanking (bull-horn), proxy attacks, sabotage, as well as psychological attacks.

As with conventional warfare, different scenarios play out:

- Attack, subdue, and conquer.
- No retreat, no surrender (*he who fights and runs away lives to fight another day*).
- Go the whole hog (*all-the-way*).
- Strategic withdrawal and re-launch of offensive.

On the surface, a corporate environment is expected to be a demilitarized zone (DMZ), one devoid of warfare. The truth however is that there's always a cold-war of competition and domination brewing underneath the apparent bonhomie.

If you've been trained that you and your colleagues are a part of a team, belonging to the bigger corporate family, naturally it would appear strange and unusual to find people being hostile, simply because it doesn't fit into the "corporate family" image you've been sold.

Remember, you're dealing with different kinds of people with religious, political, sexual orientation, and other socio-cultural views that differ from yours.

What you consider ethical and morally right will often be at variance with those of a lot of your "*corporate family*" members. While you may have bought into the "family" or "team" values preached during induction and management training sessions, and have vowed to work within those values, others may not.

They might still be clinging to the "compete-to-get-ahead" mind-set they were taught in the higher institution. You'd do well to be prepared when your so-called "*corporate family*" members do things to frustrate your efforts. The simple truth is, to such folks, you're a competitor - an obstacle to their getting ahead!

Again, don't be surprised if you find things playing out along ethno-tribal, racial, religious, political, and gender bases.

How then do I survive in this kind of environment? You might be troubled enough to ask.

Well, I've got good news for you!

This book is designed with a mind of equipping you with the relevant corporate munitions you require to survive the glass-brick-steel-and-mortar jungle your new workplace could turn out to be.

In the subsequent sections, you'll learn relevant time-tested lessons on the strategic and tactical munitions options from which you could deploy to survive the corporate cold-war jungle.

You're welcome to the corporate battle-front!

LESSON #1

YOU NEED PRAYERS FOR INSPIRATION

There's a limit to what your knowledge, skill, and experience can do. When you've exhausted your physical and mental abilities, and you're at your wit's end, you need prayers to inspire you on the way forward.

You must pray for divine direction and intervention in your sojourn through the corporate front-line.

Never leave God out of the equation. Regardless of your religious inclinations, prayer and meditation will open your eyes to see what you need to do to resolve issues and move ahead.

Please note that while it is good to pray, you must back up

your prayer with thinking; then you act when you're inspired on what to do in resolving issues that have to do with your survival in the corporate war theatre.

Believe me, it's a war and you need divine direction and intervention to survive!

LESSON #2

ALWAYS PUT ON YOUR THINKING CAP

Working in an organisation is not just about having a place to go in the morning and receiving a pay-check at the end of the month.

Companies are set up to profitably provide solutions to customers' problems. To do this, they employ people who they believe are qualified to come up with alternative options for solving these problems.

Given the above scenario, you must know that you were employed to exercise your mental capability to meet customers' expectations as a solution provider, through a series of inter-related operational processes and procedures.

To contribute to these processes, it's important that you have the capacity to think and suggest solutions, if you find favour and get involved in the planning and execution processes.

Your ability to provide excellent service/product solutions to your customers is an on-going process. To do this consistently, you must keep thinking and doing things for its benefit on a daily basis.

Make it a habit to think about things that could, in the long run, provide mutual benefit to all stakeholders - your customers, your employers, the suppliers, contractors, the government, yourself, and affiliated service providers.

LESSON #3

FIND OUT ABOUT PROSPECTIVE EMPLOYERS

It is often said that information is power. When you have more information than your peers, you have more confidence to talk about issues than they do.

This too applies to the job hunt. You must seek and obtain relevant information about prospective employers. This gives you a better insight into the companies' affairs and confidence to face up to an interview panel. This, to a certain extent, gives you a better chance of getting employed faster than your uninformed peers. Although other factors come into play in the employment process, having more information than your peers stands you in good stead than them.

Today's generation is luckier as regards getting basic information about prospective employers. All you have to do is get online and use any of the internet search engines like Google, Bing, Yahoo, AOL, Ask, and My Websearch and pronto, you are bombarded with more information than you could probably cope with. It's up to you to select and get information relevant to your immediate needs.

You must try to find out about the company's line of business other key players in the industry, its principal officers, key financial indicators its CSR projects its vision as well as long-term plans.

As regards the principal officers, being a prospective employee, you must try to have a visual image of the CEO and that of the officer responsible for your likely functional unit e.g. production, manufacturing, marketing, finance legal, etc.

Let's take it a scale up. There have been instances of CEO'S posing as gatemen (in full uniform!) during recruitment exercises to obtain on the spot information about prospective employees!

We've also had CEO'S blending into the crowd of applicants for similar reasons.

There's the story told of a military Head of State who dressed in mufti and mixed with the crowd waiting for the bus at one of his country's local bus-stops (of course, his security staff were in the crowd!).

Apparently, because they were used to seeing him in his military uniform, no one in the crowd was able to ID him. As usual in public transport, the passengers were quick to vent their frustrations on and blame the government at the least opportunity when some over-zealous traffic warden obstructed the flow of traffic. They blamed the plight of the average citizen on the insensitivity of the government.

The military head of state was glad he took the bus-ride. He was able to get first-hand information on the feelings of the people upon whom he ruled! He was sad however, because no one suggested solutions for the way forward; they were all good at analyzing the problems.

Aren't we all guilty of that? He mused.

The lesson of the story is, if anyone was planning a mutiny or insurrection against the government, he had an opportunity of getting an on-the-spot hint of it. Again, if his government was doing okay, he also had a chance of knowing that. He was saved the discomfort of having to validate the veracity of reports of sycophants!

This also applies, as with most corporate management issues, to your new work environment. Watch the things you say. There're always men-pleasers who make up for their performance and other job-related inadequacies by reporting others to get a lift.

I've got good news for you though. The basic customer service trick should get you through: be pleasant to people you meet; smile, maintain eye-contact, and say 'Hello', 'Hi', 'Good day', or whichever courtesy lingo is operational in your clime. Don't engage in a discussion about what you do not have authentic facts.

Don't play the judge; don't rubbish your co-workers, especially your superiors!

LESSON #4

BE READY TO LEARN AND ADAPT TO THE COMPANY STRUCTURE

In every work environment there is always a structure, those written and, by implication, those you're expected to learn and adapt to.

Recognize and respect the authority hierarchy and reporting lines.

Recognize and adapt within the work structure, how and when to do what is expected of you in the day-to-day operations of your employers.

Respect your reporting timeline; obey meeting rules, recognize and adapt to work flow sequence among the different functional units of the organization.

Don't get carried away by people who may tell you that there is no structure or system. There's always a structure. How it is operated is a different matter entirely.

It is up to you to ask questions about how the structure works and how to fit in. Questions like "who do I report to?" might be a good point at which to start.

When you discover who, then get in touch with the officer and let him/her show you the ropes.

Don't be surprised too to hear stuff like "I've been in the system before you came", even from staff very low down the line.

Take it in your stride. As they say in Yorubaland, "w'oju ile". It's your duty to learn as much as you can from such folks. It's also your duty to attempt to enlighten them that it's not by length of time, but by the stuff you've got packed on your top-side.

And for those who fail to develop themselves to improve their capacity or competitive advantage for advancement, you owe them the duty of genuine humane counselling on the way out of their frustration.

This will open their eyes to know that rather than take it out on you and on other new, but more qualified staff, they need to work on themselves to get ahead and enjoy the benefits that accrue to such efforts.

All you need is patience and willingness to accommodate others, teach, and also learn from them.

LESSON #5

PUT IN THE HOURS

As a newcomer, you must remember you're on an all-eyes-on-me mode. In other words, you're carrying a watch-my-every-step tag. Everyone's watching you – your punctuality, your level of diligence, attitude to delegated assignments, as well as your interpersonal relationship.

Do what is expected of you, how and when required. Don't play truancy; obtain permission if, for any reason, you must stay away from work. Follow laid down rules to obtain such permission.

You must have it at the back of your mind that virtually everyone is like let's-watch-wait-and-see-how-this-one-turns-out!

In all sincerity, recommendations about your performance will ultimately come from your line manager. However, be assured that his recommendation will be influenced by others within and outside your department, who have you under the radar.

This group of observers includes staff, as diverse and low down the pyramid, as the gateman, cleaners, and the receptionist, all of who notice your punctuality and general attitude.

Never look down on them; they may appear unlearned, but they've got common-sense! Again, I say don't look down on them. You never know who will put in a word for you!

Be willing to change your thinking.

LESSON #6

FALL IN LINE: LEARN AND ADOPT THE CULTURE

One undeniable fact is that all you know are the theoretical principles of your core profession and possibly a spattering of management principles, or as with most graduates, none at all.

Now, here comes the real deal, and you must be fast to log on to this.

Be humble enough to leave your theoretical principles at the gate and prepare your mind to learn the practical principles of "*how things are done here*", that is, the organizational **culture**.

Keep those theories and principles in the cooler, keep them and bring them to use only when you are required to do so by your superiors. Don't put on the "I know how to do it" or "I can do it better than you" garb. There's always time for that.

Your primary concern as a new team member should be to get absorbed into the main-stream of action. Therefore, you must go in as you are; learn to blend into scene, and go with the flow.

You would do yourself a world of good by putting on the *"doing-what-I'm-told"* attire, at least at the initial stages.

That way, you automatically warm yourself into the hearts of your superiors. Note however, that when in the *"doing-what-I'm-told"* mode, ensure you're always on the side of the laws and regulations of the land and within the ambits of the corporate code of ethics and conduct of your employers.

Then, you could get into the "there's got to be a better way" mode as you try to make adaptations to the way things are done.

Expect lots of taunts (overt or masked) because you are most likely to say or do some things which no induction training could take away from you.

They are those habits, opinions and values of yours which you have acquired over the years and unto which you still hold.

You may have to unlearn them and learn the new values and cultures of your new employers.

In addition, you'd discover the existence of alliances along ethnic, racial, religious, educational, political, family background, and sexual orientation bases.

Please be objective and wary of your affiliations and be guided by your long-term career development aspirations within and outside the organisation.

LESSON #7

KNOW YOUR COMPANY'S KEY FINANCIALS

Nowadays, most companies have an online presence which contains basic information about them.

This often includes key financial indices, for publicly quoted companies as well as for some limited liability companies. The fact that you are not an accountant or a financial expert is no excuse for not getting acquainted with such information.

The indicators of an organization serve as an index of its state of health. You wouldn't want to be caught napping. You're expected to know the viability and ability of your company to stay in existence and continue to meet your financial and other rewards in exchange for services rendered.

Make every effort to find out this information about prospective employers. In addition, your quest for this information must continue even after you might have joined the company. This way you'd be well informed as regards the security of your job.

According to Robert Kiyosaki (Author of "*Rich Dad, Poor Dad*"), you need to have an idea about the following financial ratios:

Gross margin percentage

Gross margin is sales minus the cost of goods sold. Gross margin percentage is the gross margin divided by sales, which tells you what percentage of sales is left after deducting the cost of the goods sold.

How high the gross margin percentage needs to be depends on how a business is organized and the other costs it has to support. For instance, after calculating gross margin percentage, the company still had to pay the workers, the utilities, the taxes, rent, and a list of other expenses.

The company also had to have enough left over to have a good return on its original investment.

Net operating margin percentage

This ratio tells you the net profitability of the operations of a business before you factor in your taxes and cost of money.

Earnings Before Interest and Taxes (EBIT) is your sales minus all the costs of being in business, not including capital costs (interest, taxes, and dividends).

The ratio of EBIT to sales is called the net operating margin percentage. Businesses with **high** net operating margin percentages are typically **stronger** than those with a low percentage. The higher the better!

Operating leverage

Every business has fixed costs that must be accounted for in the overall cost structure. The percentage of fixed costs is called operating leverage, and is calculated by dividing contribution by fixed costs.

Contribution refers to the gross margin (sales minus cost of goods sold) minus variable costs (all costs that are not fixed costs that fluctuate with sales).

Examples of fixed costs are labor related to full-time employees and most costs related to your facilities. This is what most people call overhead.

A business that has an operating leverage of 1 is generating just enough revenue to pay for its fixed costs. This would mean that there is no return for the owners. Anything over 1 is indication of profit; again, the higher the better.

Financial leverage

Almost every business needs to borrow money in order to operate. Financial leverage is a ratio that refers to the degree a business uses borrowed money. Total capital employed is the accounting value of all interest-bearing debt (leave out payables for goods to be resold and liabilities due to wages, expenses, and taxes owed but not yet paid), plus all owners' equity.

For instance, if you have $50,000 in debt and $50,000 of shareholder's equity, your financial leverage would be 2 (or $100,000 divided by $50,000).

Each business type has different standards for what a healthy financial leverage is. Other factors, such as cash flow and cost of debt, play a big part in the overall picture of financial health.

Generally, a capital-intensive company like those in the energy, oil and gas industry, marine and aviation services, require financial input by private and public investors as well as syndicated loans to meet initial capital needs.

Consequently, they have what is called a high financial leverage because the borrowed money is higher than its equity (business owners' contribution) as compared to that for companies in the fast-moving-consumer-goods (FMCG) sector, which are described as having a low financial leverage.

Total leverage

This represents the total risk that a company carries in its present business. Total leverage tells you the total effect a given change in the business should have on the equity owners. Total leverage is calculated by multiplying the operating leverage by the financial leverage.

If you are looking at the stock market, total leverage will help you decide whether or not to invest in a company. A well-run, conservatively managed company usually keeps the total-leverage **under 5.**

Debt-to-equity ratio

This one is pretty self-explanatory. It's the measure of the portion of the whole enterprise (total liabilities) financed by outsiders in proportion to the part financed by insiders (total equity).

Most businesses try to stay at a ratio of one-to-one or below. Generally speaking, the lower the debt-to-equity ratio, the more conservative the financial structure of the company.

Quick and current ratios

Quick and current ratios tell you whether or not the company has enough liquid assets to pay its liabilities for the coming year. If a company doesn't have enough current assets to cover its current liabilities, it is usually a sign of impending trouble.

On the other hand, a current ratio and a quick ratio of **2 to 1**, is more appropriate.

Return on equity

Return on equity is often considered one of the most important ratios. It allows you to compare the return a company is making on its shareholders' investments compared to alternative investments.

What do these ratios tell me?

Rich dad taught to always consider **at least three years** of these figures. The direction and trends can tell you a lot about a company and its management, and even its competitors.

Many published company reports do not include these ratios and indicators. You could calculate them when they aren't provided.

However, these cannot be used in a vacuum. They are indicators, but they must be considered in conjunction with analysis of the overall business and industry. By comparing a three-year worth of data with that of **other companies in the same industry**, you can quickly determine the relative strength of a company.

While the ratios may appear complicated at first, you will be amazed at how quickly you can learn to analyze a company. One fun exercise is to download the financial statements of public companies and run these ratios yourself. Learn how to find the information you need and see what you can learn.

Remember, these ratios are the language of a sophisticated investor. By educating yourself and becoming financially literate, you too can learn to "speak in ratios."

LESSON #8

IDENTIFY MENTORS AND LEARN FROM THEM

Having a mentor in your workplace is worth giving a consideration. It does not necessary mean kissing ass or engaging in eye-service.

You are only as wise and effective as your years of experience. You need to learn from those who have been through what you are now going through, and who definitely have more experience.

They know where the pits and the banana peels are, because they have travelled that road before you.

One of the directors at my former place of work, used to tell us back then that it is better to learn from other people's mistakes than to learn from yours.

Therefore, if you pick the right mentors, and stay close to them, you could learn a lot from their experiences.

A mentor teaches you quickly things that would otherwise have taken a longer time to learn. Beyond question, your line manager qualifies as the first mentor.

He/she is the one saddled with the responsibility of helping you grow within the organization as you contribute to the success of his unit. Failure on his part to carry out this role would most likely tell on the unit's performance.

To complement the mentoring role of your line manager, you could also have additional mentors from the different units to give you a lock-stock-and-barrel guidance about the organization.

Please note that you'd encounter some mischievously wicked supervisory and line managers who believe that since they suffered to get to where they are today, you too must go through the process!

They'd rather you steamed in your own stew than help.

People like that may never be willing to show you the ways except you're willing to kiss ass!

However, I must quickly point out that there still exist some people with the milk of human kindness, who believe you don't have to suffer as they suffered to succeed. These people, in their wisdom know you don't necessarily need to re-invent the wheel.

These are the ones to whose bosoms you must latch on, and suck as much from that milk as you can. Desire and tap into this kindness to grow at the early stages before you learn how to deal with the meat and bones of corporate workings.

Two persons that readily come to my mind regards mentoring

are Mrs. Folusho Odeyemi and Mrs. Titi Owolabi.

While Mrs. Odeyemi was my teacher at St. John's Grammar School, Oke-Atan, Ile-Ife, Nigeria, she was also instrumental to my employment at HSSL Global, a Tourism and Hospitality outfit, in Lagos, Nigeria, where she was in charge of the Business Development unit.

Likewise, Mrs. Owolabi played a key role in my foray into the Aviation Ground Support Services Industry in Lagos, Nigeria, after my stint as lesson teacher to her agile and inquisitive daughter.

Both women played, and are still playing mentoring roles of inestimable value in my life. They both qualify as my "*men-ahead*", or what the military call *point-man*. They both allowed me to latch on to their bosoms and suckle from their milk of experience.

They gave my life a new meaning; they both know we don't have to re-invent the wheel and they acted in that regard, and in my case, eliminated what could have been the beginning of a cycle of poverty, if they hadn't come along when they did.

They're both contributors to one of the platforms from which

I operate today and write books.

I must say I'm not surprised they're both making impressive progress in their respective endeavours today; they both believe that others deserve to make progress.

I'd like to add that the prayers, goodwill, and projection of the good wishes of their beneficiaries towards these women will keep lifting them, and they shall keep soaring like the eagle on the platform of their labour of love.

LESSON #9

LEARN TO SUPERVISE YOURSELF

One of the hallmarks of being an effective manager is the ability to first manage yourself. Your ability to work with minimal supervision as a neophyte, will serve to tell your supervisor that you have the potential for being a responsible manager.

Another plus in your favour would be your ability to take initiatives. However, this must not be done in isolation; you must carry your supervisor/manager along. You need his/her blessing to push your ideas through to implementation. Always remember: give no room to pride as it could spell frustration to your absorption and growth in the organization.

Learn to carry out your roles as a responsible staff, that doesn't always need to be told what to do at all times be it self-initiated roles, or those assigned by your supervisor.

Put in a good day's job. Do what is expected of you at the appropriate time. Don't steal your employer's time.

Don't forget; add an acceptable level of innovation to your roles. Do the unexpected, but within your company's code of conduct and overall business vision.

This should get your line manager to have more confidence

in you as a staff who doesn't deserve to be micro-managed.

LESSON #10

BE CAUTIOUS ABOUT DISCUSSING POLITICAL ISSUES

You're paid by your employers to think and solve problems for your customers, earn revenues, cut costs, as well as earn a good image while doing this.

It's not expected of you to turn the office into an arena for discussing local, national or global politics.

While it's okay to be politically aware, the office is hardly a place to turn into a political debate studio.

In the digital age of private blogs and vlogs where anyone could post what catches his/her fancy, there is a high tendency for misinformation.

Consequently, you may consider taking a dose of patience-and-caution pill before giving your opinion about unfolding political issues gleaned from the social media.

You could end up discovering at a later date that you've been discussing what may not have taken place at all. Believe me, you'd wish you could swallow your words if you've been hasty in giving an opinion based on misinformation.

Having said that, let me add; if you must discuss politics, I'd rather you suggested solutions to the way forward than engaging in the blame-game and heaping of insults on your leaders.

You could go a step further by putting your thoughts, frustrations, and concerns in writing to opinion leaders or your local representative in government, who is duty-bound to get your suggestions across to the policy-formulating and decision-making body in government.

Also remember this; while discussing politics, focus on suggesting solutions to issues you perceive could affect your organisation, and by inference, your livelihood!

It may interest you to know that you could hardly imagine the intrigues and under-hand scheming that take place in the local, national and global political battle-front.

Consequently, a little bit of caution will do you a world of good. I'd rather you focused on thinking of how to bring solutions to your company's customers' issues and expectations.

LESSON #11

PUT UP YOUR GUARDS AND BE ON TOP OF YOUR GAME

It is an inevitable fact that people will try to take advantage of your shortcomings or weaknesses to test you, either to embarrass you or genuinely test your competence. This is the real deal; there's no hiding place.

If you obtained your certification through fraudulent or corrupt means, this is the time you'd get exposed and ridiculed.

God be your help if you have a superior who rightly or wrongly assumes you've come to take over his/her job!

Consequently, you must be alert to avoid being taken advantage of. Work on your strengths, and capitalize on them, to minimize the exposure of your weaknesses.

Don't get carried away by the apparent camaraderie around you. Never let down your guards!

Remember, there'll always be people who will provoke you, even when, to you, there's no apparent reason for that.

However, you must realize that you're viewed as competition because formal training conditions employees' minds to compete against one another to get to the top, rather adopt the military approach of working together to beat the enemy. Thus, bear in mind you're viewed as a threat, even if you fail to regard yourself as being one.

Some even go on the offensive even if you don't have any evil scheme against them. They believe in drawing you out to do battle, even when you'd rather collaborate with them to move the organisation forward.

Those ones believe in two maxims:

- Take the battle to the enemy's territory.
- Attack is the best form of defense.

Here, it's not unusual for you to be subject to direct attacks, in form of intimidation, as well as psychological warfare to dehumanize you, and kill your drive.

You'd do well to get ready for the blame-game too! Someone somewhere is always on the look-out for a scapegoat – the guy to take the blame when the sh*t hits the fan, and things go awry.

Rather than find solutions to the issue at hand, the search light is deployed at making someone the fall-guy; it doesn't matter even if he/she has not had anything to do with the issue at hand.

You equally need to be on the look-out for people who would

try to make a fool of you or bamboozle you! It still beats me why they do this, but it does happen.

What I find most disturbing is the postulation that some superiors use it as a basis for assessing subordinates for promotion!

Well, I'd say that's primitive and negative. I don't see how a unit can work together and achieve exploits if their supposed leader is involved in head-banging!

Consequently, you need to be up to date in your assignments and reporting timelines, be ready to stand by your actions, and justify all actions you take in your line of duty. Of course, it's important for all your actions to be within the expected limits of the law and corporate code of conduct.

In addition, your humility, patience, tact, and your ability to go with the flow and persistently work hard in a smart way, will make a way for you out of the hostilities.

Note however, that you have the right to seek counsel from the Legal department or your family lawyer if you have any cause to suspect any threat to your well-being.

The other option, and a more sensible one, is to adopt the human preservation instinct;

seek greener pastures elsewhere. Leave those who want to get killed over someone else's property to do battle.

LESSON #12

CORPORATE POLITICS IS REAL: LEARN TO PLAY THE GAME

One of the initial culture shocks experienced by corporate neophytes is office politics.

Coming from a relatively academic background - *the ivory tower* - many new employees experience the baptism of corporate politics which would lead to confusion, anger and discouragement.

This often happens primarily because most new employees come in with the naive *I-don't-play-politics* mind-set.

However, the smart ones are quick to find out that they could "*play the game*" in an objective and tactful manner.

As a new employee in your new environment, you must learn the art of effective communication, the key tool of office politics.

Learn to listen more than you talk. Keep your eyes and ears wide open and your mouth closed.

Observe happenings around you, meditate, and analyse to make appropriate interpretations.

Some of the things you'd discover, if you pay adequate attention, include the fact that corporate politics involve half-truths, dummy-truths, true-lies, outright deception, distortions, manipulation, arm-twisting, blackmail, and wild-goose-chase provoking statements.

It could be a wild jungle of mumbo-jumbo, but you can survive by constant alertness and uncanny ability to listen, analyse, and interpret before taking appropriate action.

How do I avoid these? You might be tempted to ask.

My answer: you don't and can't avoid them, you go through them; you go with the flow; you play the game! Don't play dirty though! Rather than play the politics of deception, play the politics of truth. Tell the truth always - no one will kill you for that - let the deceivers keep telling lies and keep wondering what you're up to!

First, learn to keep quiet, listen, both to spoken words

and body language. You analyze what you hear with respect to body language and facts known to you.

Then you act, in words and in action.

Please don't get involved in negative politicking which could hinder your progress on the long-run because it only has short-term benefits.

Finally, because you are in a new environment, you need loads of patience to get on the same wave length with the existing staff.

Corporate politics exists in all organizations. You can't exclude yourself from it. You must learn to play the game.

There are no permanent friends or foes.

Your aspirations for quick integration, growth and career development must be at the back of your mind. However, don't engage in counter-productive politics.

You must learn very early to identify and get close to mentors who could guide and put you through.

You'd quickly learn from them the dos and don'ts of the game. Your alliances must be carefully picked and developed across board.

LESSON #13

RESPECT PEOPLE ACROSS BOARD

You must realize no two human beings have the same attitudinal and behavioural tendencies.

The work place is where you spend the most part of your days - at least 5 days a week. Consequently you are exposed to people from different background, with beliefs and values which are more often at variance with yours.

To survive your new corporate battle-field with its various attitudinal and behavioural mixes, you must unleash the tested and trusted human-attraction weapon of respect. Mark you, respect is not just something you talk about; it involves walking the talk as the saying goes.

Respect yourself; respect others including their sexual orientation, religion, political ideologies, and personal health issues.

Two key issues that often bring about debate are politics and religion; most recently sexual orientation has joined the topics of debate.

It would be nice if you avoid joining the fray; don't turn the office into a debate zone for these issues. Don't put down other people's opinion on them either. Learn to do to others what you'd like them do to you.

Learn to comport yourself with dignity and avoid being repulsive in words and action towards your co-workers.

An African adage goes:

"If you know how to comport yourself, you will be welcome in the gathering of elders"

One of the tricks of enjoying and always being welcome in the company of elders and superiors is to listen, observe, analyse, keep quiet, and only speak when called upon to do so.

It all boils down to showing respect to those who are older than you in the game.

Experience comes with how long and how well you've carried out an activity. Consequently, those who have been in the organisation longer than you, most likely, know more than you do.

If you could only learn how to show them respect, you'd open the doors to learning from them.

On the other hand, if you carry the air of "*I too know*", the "*elders*" will slam shut, the door of learning against your face.

Consequently, instead of learning quickly from their experience, you're faced with the rigor of learning slowly from your own experience.

This definitely will have its side-effect on your career development while you're still with the organisation.

It is also said: "*...respect begets respect...*" Not only must you respect your superiors, you must put aside that cocky attitude, if you've got one, and respect people 360 degrees; that is, at all levels - your colleagues, subordinates - in addition to your superiors.

If you respect people at all levels, they will respect you in return.

More importantly, you must learn to respect yourself; if you don't, you'll have problems getting others to respect you.

LESSON #14

UPDATE YOUR KNOWLEDGE ABOUT YOUR NEW EMPLOYERS

While it is very important to obtain information about your prospective employers before you join them, it is even more important that you continuously update that information as soon as you come on board.

You could do this by asking questions relevant to your needs, reading the newsletter, and gleaning information from the notice board.

As regards asking questions, you must drop your introvert-garb if you are one. Never be afraid to ask questions, even if people prove to be difficult, un-cooperative or make fun of your questions.

You must keep asking until you obtain answers to issues

troubling you; this way you won't be in the dark.

LESSON #15

DO WHAT YOU'RE TOLD

As a neophyte in your new work environment the fastest way to learn and warm your way into the hearts of the existing staff, particularly your line manager, is to do what you are told and do it how and when required, provided it's not illegal.

This to a superior and to your colleagues is a sign of obedience and willingness to learn. More specifically it is a sign that you are likely not going to be a rebel. No superior wants to have a counter-productive rebel on his hands, in addition to the troubles of managing his day-to-day operations.

If you must be a workplace rebel, your rebellion must be productive, in the interest of the corporate vision and for the benefit of all stakeholders.

However, you must first learn the rope - the way things are done in your new environment before introducing productive rebellion on a better way forward, what some call the paradigm shift.

I, must quickly point out that while it is good to do what you are told always remember that whatever you do must be within legal limits, the corporate vision and within expected standard of behavior, the code of conduct.

LESSON #16

FIND AND OPERATE WITHIN YOUR LEVEL

There is a hierarchy in every structured organization; you have your superiors, colleagues, and subordinates. Quickly discover and differentiate the three.

A quick recognition of the different existing hierarchy levels will assist you in building appropriate relationships across board.

As a graduate of a tertiary institution, some level of "executive behavior" is expected of you. It is quite different from being cocky; it requires you to exhibit a high level of self-esteem, dignity, and decorum.

Please note that this expected standard of behaviour does not preclude you from relating with your sub-ordinates. It only requires you to respect yourself when dealing with them so that they too will give you due respect. Don't engage in any form of harassment or untoward amorous behavior.

Same applies to your superiors; you must display a high level of self-respect and not turn yourself into a "kiss-ass" to get favours.

Just do your job how and when it is expected of you; that automatically earns you respect as a responsible staff. Eye-service doesn't pay on the long-run; at best it gives flash-in-the-pan benefits in the short-run because, a smart superior will eventually see through the smoke-screen.

The trick is respect yourself and respect people 360° ⁻ your superiors your colleagues, and your subordinates.

LESSON #17

AVOID BEING A NUISANCE

You have a duty post. You have a job to do; stay at your work station. Don't gallivant. If must go to the work station of other staff, keep it official, do what you need to do, without taking too much of the staff's time, and get back to your work station.

This applies too, if you have to go outside your unit to staff in other functional units.

Please note that this does not mean you turn into a mechanical worker; there is provision for a modest exchange of pleasantries and words of motivation.

Having said that, now let's come back to your inter-relationship with staff in your functional unit.

You must also avoid being a nuisance, not only in your action, but in your words as well; watch the things you say.

Words are like bullets, which once fired, don't stop until they hit a target, intended or unintended.

In Yorubaland of Nigeria, it is said, words are like a broken egg which is difficult to re-assemble; don't say things that you'd later wish you never said.

Don't say or do things that could distract your fellow staff from effectively performing their duties.

LESSON #18

DON'T BE A TOXIC STAFF

You need to make every effort to become quickly integrated into the system. Consequently, you can't afford to exhibit a disagreeable behavior in your dealings with fellow staff.

While it is okay to air your views - particularly divergent ones - avoid being overly critical of fellow staff or decisions. Learn to be objective in your views by trying to see the other side of the issue at stake.

People with a toxic disposition are, in most cases, avoided like a plague. Believe me; you don't want to be that person, because it means being quickly sidelined and only given mundane roles to play.

This could degrade to the extent you're rendered redundant and tactically eased out of the system.

Finally, as regards social integration, you could be systematically side-tracked in the social scheme of things.

LESSON #19

KEEP IT OFFICIAL

While it is okay to make the work-place less formal and more fun, learn to keep things official. Don't get overly informal or too relaxed to the extent you divulge your personal and private details.

At the same time avoid probing into other people's privacy. This could be used against you in the future by the mischievous ones.

Always remember, you're in a corporate battle field where people capitalize on your perceived weaknesses.

Remember, some over-bearing supervisors with a bullying disposition may want to twist your arm to make you divulge personal detail. This could result from a perceived notion that such supervisor has a say in your progress in the organization.

While this may be true, it is an aberration for any supervisor to act outside normally and ethically acceptable code of conduct. Not to mention going as low as blackmailing or intimidating a subordinate to divulge private information.

Don't be intimidated. In the event that you notice any form of intimidation, you have the right to report such untoward behaviour to the appropriate authorities. Remember; keep your private life private.

You must always bear in mind that you have the right to your privacy. Such disposition even makes people respect you the more. It gives them the assurance that not only will you respect their own privacy, but also the oath of confidentiality of the organisation.

Even if your line manager asks questions that infringe on your right to privacy, you have the option and owe it a responsibility to yourself not to divulge private information.

Politely, you could say: "I'd rather not discuss that" or "I'm afraid I can't discuss that with you". That should keep "*Nosey Parkers*" at bay.

Always remind yourself you're in a competitive environment and any secret of yours carelessly divulged could be taken advantage of and used against you.

LESSON #20

IMPROVE AND POSITION YOURSELF FOR PROMOTION

Getting into an organisation is one step, getting integrated, having sterling performance and getting career advancement is a different ball game.

It involves a process requiring you to improve and update yourself academically and professionally to cope with the day-to-day demands of your job.

It is often said that the day you stop learning, you start dying. One of the ways of learning is reading; that means lack of mental activity through reading could lead to gradual death of the mind.

Reading does to your brain what physical exercise does to your body. Reading tones your brain and enhances your alertness and reflexes.

Enroll for and take required professional exams in your field. This positions you on a pedestal for getting ahead faster than those who don't have such qualifications. This holds very true in a well structured environment.

However, you must realize and keep at the back of your mind that other factors could come into play. Your attitude, punctuality, and your relationship with your co-workers are equally important.

Nobody wants to work with someone with a toxic attitude or with an excessively bossy supervisor or a cocky subordinate.

Please note that in some climes, favoritism could also come into play. However, even where this is the case, the employee who would enjoy such benefits must have some recognised credentials, otherwise such benefits won't last long.

LESSON #21

STAY AWAY FROM INTIMATE RELATIONSHIPS

No doubt, daily interactions with others tend to arouse affectionate feelings towards one another. As a matter of fact, you probably spend more time with your colleagues than you spend with members of your family.

Consequently you tend to be closer to them and there is a high tendency and temptation to share secrets with them. Thus, there is a high probability of eventually getting down to having intimate relationships that could jeopardize your performance, as well as create interpersonal conflicts with other co-workers.

However, in recognition of the fact that genuine harmonious relationships could develop, which could lead to life-long marital commitments, not just to satisfy lustful cravings, you must draw a line between your relationship and performance of job responsibilities and expectations if you ever get in such relationship.

In addition, you should agree that if eventually your relationship leads to a marital union, it would not be ethical or wise to work in the same organisation, otherwise that would be like putting all your eggs in one basket.

Moreover, there is a high probability of mischievous staff playing you and your spouse against one another in the corporate power game.

LESSON #22

HUMILITY IS KEY

"Do you wish to rise? Begin by descending. You plan to build a tower that will pierce the clouds? Lay first the foundation of humility" - St. Augustine.

Summing it up, humility must not be deception-based or mere eye-service.

In the words of Jane Austin, *"Nothing is more deceitful than the appearance of humility. It is sometimes an individual boast"*.

Nothing puts people off from associating with a person as much as a cocky behavior does.

As a freshly mint, newly-out-of-school graduate, you could rightly feel good about yourself in a self-confident fashion. However, you must never allow your self-confidence to develop into over-confidence that could give others the impression you're one full-of-hot-air smart aleck.

Learn to tread softly. Respect the opinions of the people you met on ground. It is a sign of humility. Don't embark on an ego trip.

Be willing to listen and learn the ropes. Always get yourself prepared to give your opinion when asked.

There is always a time and season for everything. Please note that your opportunity to show and promote your ideas for a better way of getting things done will come. All you need is patience, and the ability to go with the flow in your new work environment.

This is what some describe as "*shape in or ship out*". The good news is some have taken the "*ship out*" way, going it on their own and making a success of it.

Steve Jobs, Bill Gates and a couple of others took the adventurous route, decided to "*ship out*" and made a success of their entrepreneurial adventures in the wild jungle of business enterprise.

However, they hung around long enough to learn the ropes. My advice; stay around long enough to push your idea and learn one or two lessons on how not to get burnt and get consumed in the business enterprise wilderness.

LESSON #23

THINK INDEPENDENLY, EMPATHISE AND COMMUNICATE OBJECTIVELY

It will do you a world of good to always have at the back of your mind that you're coming into an environment where exists people with mindsets formed and fixed by the environment and modified by existing corporate culture.

In order to warm yourself into the hearts of your co-workers, you have to reason independently, put yourself in other peoples' shoes and communicate objectively. Make every effort to avoid being labeled as one taking sides or belonging to a particular camp.

Learn to be fair, just, and objective in your reasoning, communication and actions as you get integrated into the system and imbibe its culture.

LESSON #24

INTRODUCE YOUR IDEAS WITH CAUTION

It is often said that the best players are the spectators. The reason for this may not be far-fetched. Spectators have a wider view of the field of play than the opposing contenders. Consequently, they have a clearer picture of what and how things could be done better.

This too applies in the work environment.

The new-comer quickly notices things existing staff haven't noticed or may have noticed, but had gotten used to. On the other hand, they may not have taken those things into consideration as being important.

Always remember that making change in the way things are being done could be one of the most difficult and frustrating ventures.

The first thing you're likely going to face is the "where-is-this-one-from" kind of opposition. Naturally and expectedly, this could lead to fear and anger.

In other words, your initial reaction is that you could lose your new-found self-confidence and then become angry that your "brilliant" idea was rejected.

It is natural. However, you need to quickly overcome the initial shock, engage and solicit for the assistance of people in the organisation who could influence and fast-track the implementation of your idea.

Get the buy-in of all who could influence or be influenced by your new idea, particularly those who derive joy in playing the *devil's advocate* - staff who are always mischievously happy and willing, either from personal selfish motivation, or as a political pawn, to shoot down your idea.

Don't be too proud to beg, if you have to. Don't go getting on a high horse; you've got to remember those famous words *"you stoop to conquer"*.

If, after having done all these, you still get stonewalled, then you should consider aborting the idea or beating a retreat to reformulate your strategic options.

Options open to you include:

- Abandon the project
- Change approach to stakeholder engagement
- Keep your idea for use at a later date in a new workplace
- Keep the idea for personal use when you start your own business.

LESSON #25

DON'T PLAY "I TOO KNOW" (ITK)

Over time, it has been proved that it could be to your advantage, as a new comer desirous of quick integration into the system, to play dumb on certain issues at least at the initial stages.

This does not mean you're an idiot. As a matter of fact, you couldn't have graduated if you were one, and none of the existing staff would imagine you to be one.

More specifically, to them keeping mum when issues are raised and talking when you are required to do so is a sign of level-headedness and trainability.

While it is a plus for you to play dumb, you must not overdo it. Some level of modesty is required; do remember to display streaks of intelligence along the way. This too, you must be modest about.

You must not show the existing staff you know too much otherwise they could dub you **ITK**. Once that happens, you would be gradually side-lined as a pompous person.

This is very true if you have among the existing staff someone who likes to impress it upon you that he/she's been around long before you ever dreamt of going to school! Such staff makes no bones about telling you over and over, he/she's your boss, and that he/she knows more than you do, and you must respect that!

The trick is learn to keep quiet, do what you are told to do within legal limits and corporate expectations, objectively analyse issues and body-speak, and act at the appropriate time.

If the outcome of your analysis doesn't add up with available facts, or the latest facts are at variance with earlier facts, then know someone is playing games with your mind.

You must not play into the hands of such fellows. Let such outcomes guide the things you say and do.

In fact, you'd be better off cultivating the habit of asking questions more than putting forward your opinion on issues, no matter how naive people claim your questions are.

When you ask questions, you receive information that improves your knowledge about your new work environment, and you get wiser on its workings.

LESSON #26

BE PUNCTUAL

Punctuality, they say, is the soul of business. While this may sound very old school to the Millennials, you can't deny the fact that going late for a crucial meeting or appointment is a sign of irresponsibility.

I realize that some people would like to argue that the important thing is to put in a good day's job and finish all assigned roles.

This could hold true where you're working solo. However, where you're working as part of a team of professionals who have specific meeting, planning, and role execution times, lateness could paint you in the negative colours of un-seriousness.

In addition, even where the flexible-hour system is being operated you're duty-bound to report at your duty post, as well as for meetings at the prescribed time.

Don't allow demoralizing agents throw cold water on your passion and desire for doing what is right and expected of you by your organization.

Don't allow ***agents-provocateurs*** mislead you into doing what is not right, and go behind to rat on you.

LESSON #27

MAKE AN IMPACT

Given that nothing lasts forever, use your time in the organisation to make a positive impact in terms of human relation and attitude towards your work, and co-workers.

Your attitude is an inner disposition reflected in your outward behavior towards people as well as towards your roles and responsibilities.

You owe it a duty to yourself for your progress and for posterity, to make a positive impact on your colleagues, subordinates and supervisors.

What you do today become tomorrow's history. Leave an indelible impact in the hearts of everyone while you're still in the organisation. This paves the way for good word-of-mouth recommendation and referrals when you need it in the future. In addition, this opens the doors to you anytime you have reason to come back to the organization in the future.

LESSON #28

PATIENCE PAYS MULTIPLE DIVIDENDS

The old saying: that "*the patient dog eats the fattest bone*" still holds true today. Over time, it has held sway and no one has been able to prove otherwise.

Don't pay attention to those who might want to stampede you into taking rash decisions by their suggestive words or by calling you names such as "snail", "slow coach", "tortoise", "millipede", "trailer", "chain-link earth-mover".

I'd like you to know that "*all is well that ends well*".

While it is true that the work place involves inter-personal competition to get ahead of your peers, you must be wary of fighting over another man's property.

Come to think of it, if you're working in a privately owned organization, and you engage in a do-or-die competition with your colleagues to the extent you go as far as consulting the occult (black magic) or spiritual powers, to get ahead of them or even un-seat your superior, what do you expect of the owner of the company?

In the words of world-acclaimed Nigerian juju musician, **Ebenezer "Obey" Fabiyi**: "*Eni ri nkan he, to fe ku pelu re*".

In other words, why would you want to kill yourself or others over what is not yours?! Why don't you learn from the words of jazz musician, **Najee** in his "Day by Day" track: *"nothing lasts forever"*, not even the post of Permanent Secretary!

Why don't you imbibe the virtue of patience, learn the ropes, develop yourself, be diligent and let your performance speak for you?

Please note that if you think you're not getting what you deserve, in view of your diligence and loyalty, start looking beyond your present work-place instead of fighting over what is not your birth-right!

I can tell you, it's not a pleasant thing to have the blood of the innocent crying out to you and tormenting you every day because you're occupying a seat for which you shed blood to capture.

LESSON #29

DON'T START WHAT YOU CAN'T SUSTAIN

Consistency of attitude, behaviour, in words and in action, is one of the attributes of great leaders.

As a graduate you're a potential leader, consequently you must not be of unstable character.

Never allow yourself to be viewed as someone who can be swayed in any direction by the whims of manipulators in the corporate power-game.

While it is good to go the extra-mile to get things done in resolving corporate challenges and external customers' issues, your actions must be sustained and not discontinued after a while. Whatever you do must not be a flash-in-the-pan stuff that could get you labeled "men-pleaser" or "Mr. eye-service".

LESSON #30

GEAR YOURSELF UP TO SOLVE PROBLEMS

You must realize from the onset that as a graduate you were employed to think and provide solution alternatives to corporate challenges and customers' problems.

Develop yourself mentally and emotionally to meet challenges head-on. Read widely and consult experienced people.

Actively seek out new technological, administrative, and management trends and adopt them in your day-to-day activities to improve operational and administrative processes.

Fortunately, this should present minimal problems since we now have access to real-time online search engines - Google, Yahoo, Ask, Web search, AOL and many others. While others complain, think about how to solve problems that could make you and your organization move forward.

Your ability to do this effectively, to some extent, paves the way for your integration and growth within the organization. Of course, other factors like your attitude and interpersonal relations and the other issues highlighted in this book, come into play.

Carry other staff, especially your line manager, along as you engage in this activity, to get their buy-in and eventual adoption across board.

LESSON #31

PRACTISE THE THREE F's

As opposed to the sexist vulgar 3-F's (Find them, Friend them, F**k them) used as regards women, the 3 F's of the corporate world encourages you to be objective in your dealings with others in line with the **Golden Rule** (*do to others what you'd like others do to you*).

You must be **friendly, fair** and **firm** in your dealings with your co-workers in a modest fashion. Seek people out, get friendly within acceptable limits, but don't mess with them or screw them up. Keep your promises, live up to your words, and don't get involved in backstabbing. Treat people how you would like to be treated (**The Golden Rule**). Don't take sides when resolving issues for any reason whatsoever. Say it the way it is without fear or favour.

Don't play to the gallery either – you don't get by for long by being a men-pleaser. It doesn't work because the truth will eventually come out. Learn to take an objective view and stand by it. People will respect you for that. A person who equivocates and engages in dilly-dally is not respected by serious-minded individuals. Don't be one!

Be friendly, fair and firm. These attributes are a sign of

leadership potential. You must from the onset exhibit these qualities in your work environment.

LESSON #32

CONSULT: YOU DON'T KNOW IT ALL

While it is true that you've gone through the higher institution and you have most probably come out with technical knowledge, you still need to consult existing staff on how things go down in your new workplace.

This applies even to technical issues because, most likely all the knowledge you have are theoretical in nature, not real-life experience.

For this, you need to consult existing staff on how things are done, which in most cases, are different from the theoretical knowledge you possess. Application of theoretical knowledge differs from one organization to the other, each has its own business and operational models which you must learn in order to operate effectively and grow.

You must be willing to ask questions about what others know that you don't know.

Don't feel too big to ask for help when you're in need of information. No one has it all; you need others to help you get what you lack, just as others need you to help them get what they don't have.

Thus, asking for help is nothing to be ashamed of, or feel too big about.

No one knows it all. Therefore, you must be open and willing to learn from the existing staff that which you don't know.

Don't feel too big to learn from experienced staff.

In addition to technical knowledge, you need to understand the intrigues, behind-the-scene power-plays, affiliations and the interest groups that could make or mar your progress if not taken into consideration.

LESSON #33

YOU NEED EMOTIONAL INTELLIGENCE

To survive the corporate jungle with its diverse occupants, you need to have and deploy the tools of emotional intelligence.

First, you must know yourself very well - your make-up. You must be aware of your passion and motivation - the things that make you want to act or make you act the way you do.

Next, you must be able to know how and when to act or refrain from acting. When you do act, you must do so objectively and rationally in every situation that presents itself. You must be able to see beyond the present moment to know the implications of your action or inaction on all parties concerned.

This requires ability to think ahead and stay level-headed even in the face of provocation and rising tension. Then, you must be empathetic, be able to put yourself in other people's shoes, to understand why they talk and act the way they do.

You must learn to listen and observe people in your new environment to be able to give appropriate reaction to their actions towards you.

You need to learn how to remain calm, put a rein on your emotions, when the inevitable fireworks start.

Finally, you must be able to use your knowledge about yourself, your passion and motivation to manage your relationship with your co-workers, based on what you know about them.

Communication skills play an important role in managing your emotions. Words have been likened to broken eggs and bullets. Broken eggs are difficult to re-assemble; bullets only stop when they hit a target. Likewise, it is difficult to take back spoken words.

People relate in the workplace mostly through spoken words, and words are the sources of most relationship issues.

Consequently, it is very crucial to put a rein on your tongue.

You could learn more through the following books:
1. "*Oops - How not to Swallow your Words*"
2. "*Watch your Words*"

They're available at the following online links:
https://www.amazon.com/dp/1495221113

LESSON #34

EXPLOIT GREEN-HORN OPPORTUNITIES

It has been observed that neophytes generally carry this aura that makes some of the existing staff sympathetic – at least to some extent at the initial stages.

They appear to welcome you into their midst, at least until reality dawns on some that "this one could be a threat to my job".

Now, don't blame anyone for feeling like that; it's a natural human survival instinct coming into play! Please note it is most likely that some just despise you from the onset.

You must try and learn as much as you can from those that accept you whole-heartedly, before you lose the aura.

Ask questions about the organization; its operation, job security, its competitors, the principal officers, the owners, its standing with the banks, legal obligations, political affiliations, social responsibility projects, existence of and relationship with the labour union, standing within its industrial sector.

This is to confirm or disprove what you've learnt about the organization through your online search.

Knowledge of the above will help you determine your next

steps in getting integrated into the system, as well as your plans for the future within and beyond the organization.

LESSON #35

LEAVE YOUR BAGGAGE AT THE GATE

The corporate environment, to some extent, is a leveler of sorts. It brings people from different background together to work under the same roof. Of course, this does not rule out the existence of "class" levels in the hierarchy structures.

However, within the hierarchy levels, different people with different background, age, religion, sexual orientation and political affiliations are brought together into the same group - factory shop-floor staff, supervisors, managers and directors.

Irrespective of your age, education or experience, you're

grouped with staff on your hierarchical level.

Given the above scenario, it would be in your interest to leave your family background status, education, age, and experience at the gate. These factors should be kept under control and never allowed to over-influence your interaction with your co-workers, your customers and suppliers/contractors.

No matter your education or years of experience, you're likely to hear the phrase: *"wait for your turn"* from the existing staff who believed you've got to go through the thresher the way they did to get to where they are.

This could be one of the culture shocks awaiting you as you blend into the new work environment, particularly coming from the higher institution with a mind-set and expectation of rapid promotion.

It's entirely up to you to decide whether you're ready to stay on the grind-mill and mark-time, while waiting for your upgrade.

On the other hand, you could consider making a move to search for greener pastures, or if you've got entrepreneurial impatience, you could move on to start your own business.

LESSON #36

RESPECT THE OATH OF CONFIDENTIALITY

Corporate information and trade secrets are jealously guarded for reasons of competitive advantage. Even when a company is publicly quoted, only some prescribed information is required to be made public.

As a responsible officer, you must keep company confidential information secret. Do not be fast with the tongue where corporate secrets are concerned.

You must respect the oath of confidentiality - both written and unwritten - which you have sworn to abide with.

Confidentiality of trade secrets and financial information becomes even more critical as regards inter-company rivalry within your company's industry.

You must be wary about what you discuss with strangers, visitors, suppliers, customers, contractors, and consultants.

You never can tell who is working underground for the competition, as these same set of people often do business with other companies, the competition inclusive!

You must remember you could be a target of colleagues or even subordinates who have no qualms about adopting unethical competitive tactics to get ahead of you.

Your ability to keep sealed lips on confidential matters places you on a pedestal of professionalism and trustworthiness.

In matters of your organisation's secrets, it is better to be dubbed a know-nothing than a quick-with-the-tongue loud-mouth!

Whereas, in your mind, you know you've taken on the role of a responsible officer who is not only informed, but wouldn't divulge official secret. Learn to keep secrets secret.

LESSON #37

AVOID EYE-SERVICE

"Not with eye-service, nor men-pleasers," - Eph. 6:6

As a fresh-out-of-school staff still hot with new ideas, what is expected of you is to work with passion to bring about changes that could move your organization forward.

Along the line, you too would wish to meet your expectations of income, promotion and career development. While it is good to be thrilled to work and advance, you must not taint your integrity with eye-service, all in a bid to get ahead of your peers.

Just do your bit, how and when expected, and be consistent in whatever you do even as you improve on the way you carry out your responsibilities.

Please note that when your effort and commitment are being recognised, some will still dub you a men-pleaser. I'd like to encourage you, not to give up being a person of integrity, a committed and loyal staff to your organization.

I would like to give you a heads-up on eye-service. Every smart supervisor or manager will recognize a subordinate that engages in this practice. Consequently, they are always on guard and are very sensitive to the hokey-pokey of such staff.

Finally, benefits derivable from engaging in eye-service often don't stand the test of time. Don't get yourself involved in it, only lazy, unserious and mischievous staff do.

LESSON #38

WORK SMART: OPTIMIZE YOUR TIME ENERGY AND MATERIAL RESOURCES

"It's not how hard you work, but how much you get done".

While some people think you must work smart and then work hard to maintain your success, others believe you must work hard to lay the foundation for working smart – getting a better way doing hard work. Irrespective of which side of the opinions you're, it is crucial to do things most relevant to your goal at the appropriate time, applying appropriate level of gumption and energy.

Learn to do what needs to be done, and do it at the right time. Do not procrastinate.

Set a list-of-what-to-do as a guide. Ensure you set goals you can achieve within a given time frame every day.

Don't leave undone till another day what you must do today. Do what must be done; do what you need to do, not what you want to do. Learn to do first things first. Avoid "busyness" without tangible result.

Your ability to do this well will get better with practice and lessons learnt over time.

Success answers to smart hard work. Hard work doesn't kill; it even strengthens and conditions your mind to appreciate success when it comes.

Go ahead and work hard in a smart way in your new environment. It's a good leverage for winning and getting ahead.

LESSON #39

PUT YOUR TALENTS TO USE

"Use what talents you possess; the woods will be very silent if no birds sang there............." - Henry Van Duke.

According to the Scriptures, the gift (talent) of a man will create opportunities for him, and bring him into the presence of important people. It's just not enough to have talents, - academic and natural - you must put them to use.

Having talents, but not putting them to use could be compared to burying them. If you do that, there is no benefit, either to you or to your co-workers and your employers.

If you have unexploited talent, you're like someone who winks in the dark, only you know what you've got going for you. You need to work on your talent and put it to use for the benefit of your co-workers and your employers for it to be of value.

Otherwise, a hard-working staff without as much talent as you possess will surpass you, and be accorded recognition and reward at your expense.

Please note that when you put your talent to work to add value to your co-workers and your company's operations as a whole, your gift is bound to make a way for you to be recognized and rewarded somehow, some day.

However, you must be ready to fight all battles against you, to protect your talent.

Please note that it's not enough just to have talent; what's more important is your ability to use your talent to add value to the quality of life of others, and by extension, your own life too.

LESSON #40

THINK BEYOND YOUR PRESENT EMPLOYER

While it is good to rejoice upon getting employed to work in your present organization, it is equally important to start making plans for your future. This includes plans for growth within the organization over the number of years you expect to stay with the employer.

Secondly, it must include what is known as retreat strategy.

While you're making in-roads as regards integration and growth within the organization, you must also have at the back of your mind, that you'll reach a point in time when the honorable thing to do is to seek new conquests elsewhere.

It could be due to the fact that you're no longer getting your expectations met in terms of growth, reward, recognition, acceptance of new ideas for better ways of getting things done or perceived foul plays, under-hand scheming, unfairness, injustice, racial/tribal discrimination and other forms of discrimination.

Your retreat strategy should be diverse and include the options like:

- Getting a better job elsewhere
- Embarking on an entrepreneurial venture

with one or two people
with whom you share
similarities.

LESSON #41

CHANGE WHAT YOU CAN

Although the only thing in life that keeps happening is change, as a new-comer in an organisation, you can't force a change, particularly if you're coming in at a middle management level.

You've got to work on it to obtain a buy-in and approval of your idea by all the relevant stakeholders. Then, you could start the implementation process, while you carry them along.

If you're in charge of a team, you must lead by example - you must first do what you want your staff to do. Let them see that you're not a slave driver who is not ready to get his hands soiled.

Roll up your sleeves and show them how you want things done! Be their champion; let them see you as someone who'd watch their back, and stand up for them!

Don't force change; let it happen naturally, particularly if you're dealing with the Millennials. These ones want to have fun while working. Consequently, you must find a fun way of getting them involved in the implementation of your new idea.

Don't give yourself hypertension over what you can't change. You can only fight what you can; you mustn't engage in a battle you know you can't win.

Remember, you too may have some shortcomings which, in your team members' point of view, need to be changed!

You must learn to engage in "give-and-take", "win-and-lose". Learn to accept new ideas from your team members too. No single team member must have his/her way all through.

There must be room for compromise in your attempt to make process and procedural changes.

Consequently, you too must be willing to change for the benefit of your team.

You must keep working on the change project while harmonizing your team's inter-relationship as well as their relationship company-wide, to attain and sustain a state of balance, because of issues that are bound to come up every day that could challenge the status quo.

LESSON #42

BE A CHAMPION OF YOUR TEAM

As a graduate, you're most likely to come in at mid-management level; this could mean you'd probably have staff reporting to you as the head of a team. Lead by example.

Display your competence by first showing them how to do what you want them to do. The worst you could do for yourself is dish out orders on what you don't know how to do.

Once they find out you're incompetent, you'll be at their mercy; because they could threaten to down tools. Please note there's a limit to which you could threaten to sanction them.

Today's generation of workers won't budge to unjust threats;

they know their rights under the labour laws.

Even if they don't down tools, they could mess up your deliverables in terms of quality, timelines, and cost.

Your presence and influence must always be felt, whether you're physically present or not. However, you must not micro-manage your team.

Managers who insist on being involved in every detail demoralize their employees, add undue stress to their own lives, and endanger their organisation's long-term success.

Nobody is born a mediocre. Everyone has the potential to be great. Motivate your team to perform using appropriate tactics. Discover and help them meet their expectations and requirements.

LESSON #43

BE ON THE SIDE OF INTEGRITY

Be known as someone who could always be trusted; be known consistently as someone whose words and promises could be relied upon.

Your integrity status must not be a one-off thing; it must be consistent. If you're known as a person of integrity, you won't give your co-workers any reason to suspect or, doubt you, or read meanings to your words and actions.

The first attribute every business man looks for in his staff is integrity. This gives your employer some level of confidence that you're less likely to fiddle with the books, than someone who is outright untrustworthy.

Integrity opens doors for you to dine at the same table with princes and nobles! Let your yea be yea and your nay be nay.

Don't make promises you can't fulfill. If you do make any promise, then try by all means to fulfill it.

If you're on the side of integrity, you'd take decisions and not lose any sleep over it because you're plain-hearted.

Always remember you're a brand that must be developed. Consequently, you must do all that's necessary to endear yourself into the hearts of your co-workers, particularly, your line manager.

Let the words of **Simon Mainwaring** be your guide:

"The keys to brand success are self-definition, transparency, authenticity and accountability".

In the business world, nobody wants to employ an unreliable person who also lacks financial responsibility and accountability.

Let everyone within and outside your workplace see and know you as a person of integrity; someone who can be relied upon enough to be trusted with money. This has long-term benefits if you plan on setting up your own business.

When you operate from the pedestal of integrity and financial probity, high net-worth individuals and investors will be willing to take a risk and put money into your business, assured they will get a reasonable return on their investment.

LESSON #44

DON'T PUT YOUR COLEAGUES DOWN

Notwithstanding the fact there's competition in most workplaces, you can't possibly do anything worse than put your co-workers down in the presence of other people.

The reason is that outsiders will treat you, your colleague, and the company in the light of how you present your co-workers to them.

The danger here is that you could unknowingly give outsiders the chance to get into your team through negative things you say about one another, probably out of anger.

Consequently, you must avoid doing this because it could bounce back at you!

Rather, you must say and do things that promote and protect your co-workers, your company, and ultimately yourself.

LESSON #45

DON'T LOOK DOWN ON ANYONE

In your interaction with your co-workers and all external customers, learn to exhibit a pleasant attitude.

Smile, maintain eye-contact, and say Hello, Hi, Good day, or whichever words of greetings are used in your work environment.

The fact that you've been through the ivory tower doesn't give you the liberty to go on an ego trip, with your nose in the air.

What you probably know is all you learnt in school, not what you're definitely going to learn in your new workplace.

I can guarantee you, your teachers in this new environment are many and diverse, including the gatemen, cleaners, office assistants, and of course your colleagues and superiors.

My advice, be humble, be open, be accommodating, and be ready to learn.

Please permit me to share with you, a story a friend told me. I hope you'd be able to relate it to the issue at hand:

Samira worked at a meat distribution factory. One day, when she finished with her work schedule, she went into the meat cold room to inspect something, but in a moment of bad luck, the door closed and she was locked inside with no help in sight. Although she screamed and knocked with all her might, her cries went unheard as no one could hear her. Most of the workers had already gone, and outside the cold room it's impossible to hear what was going on inside. Five hours later, whilst Samira was on the verge of death, the security guard of the factory eventually opened the door. Samira got miraculously saved from dying that day. When she later asked the security guard how he had come to open the door, which wasn't his usual work routine.

His explanation: "I've been working in this factory for 35 years, hundreds of workers come in and go out every day, but you're one of the few who greet me in the morning and say goodbye to me every night when leaving after work. Many treat me as if I'm invisible. Today, as you reported for work, like all other days, you greeted me in your simple manner 'Hello'. But this evening after working hours, I curiously observed that I had not heard your "Bye, see you tomorrow". Hence, I decided to check around the factory. I look forward to your 'hi' and 'bye' every day because they remind me that I am someone. By not hearing your farewell today, I knew something had happened. That's why I started searching everywhere for you.

Moral lesson of the story: Be humble, love and respect those around you. Try to have an impact on the people you come across every day, you never know what tomorrow will bring.

LESSON #46

MANAGE INTER-PERSONAL RELATIONSHIPS

Given that you're in an environment made up of people with different attitudinal and behavioural make-up, people are bound to step on each other's toes once in a while in line of duty.

Learn to admit your mistakes, apologise, and correct them.

Nothing douses tension between two enraged party more than one party backing down and saying: "*I'm sorry*".

No one is perfect. Be humble enough to say "I'm sorry". Don't be too proud to beg.

"A man must be big enough to admit his mistakes, smart enough to profit from them, and strong enough to correct them". – John C. Maxwell.

Don't give room to hard-feelings towards you by your

co-workers. Ask for forgiveness when you're wrong.

You and I are human; we're prone to making mistakes. No one is perfect. One of the beauties of life, and of divine magnanimity is that, very often, we get the chance to learn from our mistakes. This means we often have the chance to guard against future occurrence.

Learn to own up to your mistakes and make corrections. Doing this doesn't subtract anything from your person; rather it helps improve your inter-personal relationship with your co-workers.

Don't feel too big to accept your mistakes. Such behaviour reeks of pride, and if it persists, could jeopardise your integration and career development.

One certain and undeniable fact is that your future starts from day one and how you manage relationships with your co-workers.

It's entirely up to you to avoid issues that could lead to a breakdown of your relationship with your co-workers. Learn to own up to your mistakes and correct them!

While it is a great sign of humility to apologise and beg for forgiveness, to forgive is an act of divine kindness. You too must learn to forgive your co-workers when they ask for forgiveness.

If you forgive your co-worker when he/she asks for forgiveness, you free him/her from guilt. Likewise, you set yourself at liberty from the grudge virus, and heart-ache!

Don't bear grudges against your co-workers. Don't give room for ill-will in your interpersonal relationship with them. Forgive, get the issue behind you and forge ahead together towards your career objective.

LESSON #47

EFFECTIVE COMMUNICATION IS IMPORTANT

In the business world, virtually all interactions are based on communication with words or symbols.

The role of communication is crucial in getting ideas, feelings, opinions, and thoughts across to co-workers – colleagues, superiors, and subordinates – and the external customers of your employers.

It is equally important in resolving issues that are bound to arise in the course of your workplace interactions – group conflicts, labour issues, corporate politics, etc.

It is your duty to ensure that every stakeholder understands what information you're trying to pass across. Even when messages are encrypted or coded, they must be appropriate such that the receiver will be able to decode it. This is to avoid the negative after-effect that miscommunication could have on the interpersonal relationships within and outside the organisation.

Learn to say the relevant things as the occasion demands. Use appropriate communication tools, modes, and models as are relevant to the business environment in which your company operates.

In the business world, effective communication is critical, from spoken words to written documents; it is believed that a manager spends up to 70 - 90 percent of his time engaged in one form of communication or the other.

This includes formal communication, in form of business documents like contract agreements, official letters, as well as informal communication such as the grapevine, which must not be under-rated.

You must also be aware of unspoken words – you must be able to *"read between the lines"*.

Learn to interpret body language, signs, and symbols too.

In addition, you must know how to say the right words at the appropriate time. Guard your mouth and speak because you have something to say, not because you have to say something.

Let your words, in plain or masked language, match the occasion when you're discussing with your co-workers, your team, and your company's external customers.

LESSON #48

LEARN TO SMILE

A smile is one the most potent communication tools. It speaks volumes even, when no words are uttered.

When you put up a smiling face, you re-assure everyone around you - your colleagues, customers, suppliers, contractors - that you're approachable and not in a fighting mood.

This magnetically draws people to you; and you can always get whatever you want!

Every wise woman would know that the most powerful weapon of getting what she wants from her superiors and colleagues is the smile.

She knows she can't use force to have her way with her

superiors and colleagues; it won't work!

Now, to the other side of the coin; smiling to get what you want is not reserved for the womenfolk alone. Men can also get what they want by smiling, though this may be a tough one for most men!

Learn to temper the anger with a smile. When your superiors or colleagues are angry with you, apply one the most powerful tools of providing excellent Customer Service - smile!

Now, concerning your office or business environment, be known to your colleagues, superiors, subordinates, and business associates - customers and suppliers - as a warm and approachable person.

Learn to smile when appropriate; this will help you warm your way into the hearts of others, and win them over to your side.

In my opinion, this could be the reason why English writer, Joseph Addison said:

> *"What sunshine is to flowers, smiles are to humanity; these are but trifles, to be sure; but scattered along life's pathway, the good they do is inconceivable."*

Finally, while it is good to smile always, make it a habit to follow up your smile with good deeds!

LESSON #49

DESIRE TO SUCCEED AND PURSUE EXCELLENCE

Rather than being envious or critical of those ahead of you in your workplace, desire to excel in the manner you carry out your roles, and follow up your aspiration with action.

In other words, do not just wish for success, passionately and diligently work your way to career development success.

Don't allow the spirit of fear keep you away from pursuing success through excellent disposition towards your roles and responsibilities.

Learn and do what those ahead of you did to get to where they are, and avoid those things they didn't do well.

One of the key principles of career development is clarity of purpose. This drives your vision, strategy, tactics, and actions.

When you know where you're going or where you want to get to, you will be in a better position to devise how to get there.

For instance, identifying and learning from mentors; improving your capacity through self-sponsored educational pursuit, are examples of how to get to where you've got your eyes on.

You must aspire to do more than your peers, and be ready to up the *ante* every time you've achieved a goal. Continually improve the way you carry out your roles.

LESSON #50

PURSUE A DISCIPLINED HEALTH REGIME

Your state of health determines your ability to make positive contributions to the operations of your company. Key among the things that contribute to your state of health is what you put in your mouth - foods, beverages, and drugs.

At daily recommended proportions/doses, they contribute to sound health; however, exceeding those levels could lead to adverse health issues either in the short-term or in the long run.

Eat foods that are right for your system. Watch out for how your body reacts to certain foods; then knock off your menu, those you cannot cope with.

Maintain a proper and balanced combination of carbohydrates, proteins, fats and oils, spices, vitamins, and minerals.

You must make it a point of duty to drink clean water every day, even if you're observing a fast.

As regards your duty roles, it is understood, you have to work hard to keep up with business demands; I would like to say however, that it is better to work hard in a smart way.

If you're put in charge of a team, learn to delegate. Engage your team members; let them carry out work-related roles on your behalf. If you're afraid of letting go, to the extent that you do almost everything by yourself, you will experience burn-out, with its negative health implications.

You must rest from work, as *all work and no play makes Jack a dull boy.*

Make time to relax – watch TV, listen to music, engage in leisure sports, such as golf, tennis, badminton, etc.

You must exercise – on your own, or you could join an aerobics class if time and money permit.

You must also go for medical check-up on a regular basis, to identify not-so-obvious medical conditions that could have adverse effect on your well-being and ability to keep being relevant in your workplace.

LESSON #51

DON'T CHEAT YOUR EMPLOYERS

According to the general saying:

"...what goes round comes round"

What you do today to your present employers will come back to haunt you. It's just a matter of time; the chicken will come home to roost.

Again, one of the Codes of Honour in the military is that a team member will not cheat other members and can expect that other members will not cheat him/her.

This is one of the principles that keep them together;

they're loyal to one another and are always watching out for one another.

Always do with passion, what is expected of you, how, and when expected.

Put in the hours; occupy your hours with productive and profitable activities. Do not waste your employer's time or your colleagues' time by engaging in unofficial or unproductive activities.

I would like you to know that nothing is hidden; people you least expect to be influential in your promotion are watching.

Remember, if you cheat your employer, your employees will cheat you when you start your own business.

> *"Do unto others as you would like them do unto you"*.

LESSON #52

DON'T ALLOW YOURSELF TO BE CHEATED

There are always two sides to a coin. Having cautioned you not to cheat your employers, it is equally important that I let you know that you too do not deserve to be cheated by your employers.

Whoa! Whoa! Are you telling me my employer could cheat me?! You're tempted to ask?

Right! I say, and the problem is you may never know until you're in, whether you've done due diligence or not!

In some climes, there could be officers who are supposed to be responsible for your welfare in the company and who know what you rightly deserve, but will not give it to you until you agitate for it!

Consequently, you could end up not getting what you were promised during the recruitment process, except you stand your ground and fight for it.

One way of avoiding a face-off between you and your employer is to get everything stated in black-and-white, and be conversant with the operative labour laws in your area.

Consequently, if there's a violation of terms to which you both agreed, you have a basis on which to seek redress.

If any employer is reading this, please note that today's generation of employees is more informed, restless, and aware of their legal rights.

Please don't cheat them. They'll always find a way of getting back at you!

> *"Do unto others as you would like them do unto you"*.

LESSON #53

DRESS APPROPRIATELY

In the part of Africa where I come from, it is often said:

"How you appear to people in your dressing and your comportment determines the degree of honour others give you"

You must learn to dress to fit the occasion. Dressing for work is different from that for social functions.

Nowadays, most organisations have dress codes. The dress code for the technical team is different from those in the administrative units.

As a manager-in-training, you must set the tone by being properly dressed within the ambits of the acceptable organisational dressing culture.

Otherwise, you may not be able to enforce the dress code amongst your team.

LESSON #54

LIVE WITHIN YOUR INCOME

One of the yardsticks for measuring your suitability for responsible posts and roles is your ability to manage your income. Don't be tempted to put on an air of "I've arrived" and start living beyond your financial capacity.

Learn to do a basic savings, income, and expense calculation before you receive your salary. Determine ahead what you will save and what you'll spend.

Don't be tempted to develop unrealistic spending goals. Don't make financial promises you can't keep. Don't pretend to be what you're not.

You must be realistic and let your expenses match your peculiar circumstance and background, and long-term personal and career development goals.

Determine what your income is and the things you need or must have; knock off your list what you don't need; buy things based on their order of priority and importance.

It is a crucial but tough task that requires discipline and commitment.

Differentiate between what you **need** and what you **want** or wish to have. The difference is that you could do without what you want or what you wish to have, but you can't do without what you need or what is essential to your continued existence and well-being.

What you need is a necessity or a must-have; whereas what you want is anything you wish to have probably because others have it and you're experiencing the "*I-want-to-belong*" syndrome.

Do not pretend to be whom and what you're not. Don't waste your hard-earned money trying to impress or oppress people, particularly the opposite sex.

Do not carry an air of being sophisticated if you're not, because people will soon see through the smoke-screen.

Don't live in a high-brow apartment when you should be living in a low- or medium-income flat; don't take up a multi-room apartment if what you could afford is a mini-flat or a bed-sitter. Don't be tempted to see this admonition as "poverty mentality".

Do not be tempted by those who believe "*to be rich, you must move close to the rich*". Although there could be some truth in that, the over-riding truth and reality is that you must avoid living beyond your income!

You don't necessarily have to live in the same neighbourhood with the rich and famous to become one! It is a gradual process; the truly wealthy ones, not the flash-in-the-pan nouveau-riche wannabe's, must have paid their dues, you too must pay yours! All it takes is patience and committed smart hard work on your part!

To live with the rich, you have to be able to pay the bills without being fraudulent. As a matter of fact, living in the same neighbourhood with the rich before you're ready for it could get you into the type of financial mess that could ruin you. This could happen if you keep accumulating bills that your income cannot accommodate.

Don't get carried away by what pretenders are doing thinking they're having a good time. Don't spend beyond your means; be realistic!

Please note that this does not mean you shouldn't think big or have aspirations of achieving greatness. What I'm saying is *"cut your coat according to your pocket!"* Live within your income while you desire, plan, and work hard in a smart way towards greater things.

In other words, while it's good to see the big picture, start from where you are and grow to the place you desire. When you get to the place of your dreams, you get to live at that level with all the trappings that go with that status!

Again, don't be a victim of "first-harvest" syndrome – the temptation to spend your first series of income on whatever catches your fancy!

Mark you, your first series of income could be a source of temptation to spend lavishly because of what experienced people call the **spirit of control** which they claim money tend to possess.

If you're not mindful of your habits – old and newly developed ones – money could control you. You may become tempted to spend outside your financial capacity.

If care is not taken, you could *eat up* what you could easily have turned into your business start-up capital. The sure way to overcome this *control* is to maintain, for a period of time, your *status quo antes,* – your previous status before you became employed.

Do this for **at least** six months to enable you build up your capital and consolidate your position before you gradually start doing things that match your new status. You have the liberty to choose your own timeline though.

I can tell you, there is hardly anything as embarrassing as being in a financial mess. It reduces a man to something worse than a castrated dog! It completely incapacitates and turns you to a beggarly no-choice entity; you take whatever is handed down to you.

To avoid this, you must plan how you manage your finances - income and spending.

It is very easy to get emotional with spending, but you must avoid travelling that road!

That is, you could be tempted to spend on the spur of the moment going by present-day advertising and display of goods.

Consequently, you must always be conscious and careful not to buy things you do not need. Do not follow the crowd or the hype to buy what you'd later regret you bought.

To manage your money, make provisions for:

- Your regular needs.
- Emergencies.
- Business investment opportunities.

Now, I do realise that for some people, this may be a struggle because as they say *"the take-home pay cannot even take me home!"*

The way around this is for you to learn to live within your income, and avoid the temptation to *"keep up with the Joneses"*!

For instance, don't shop at high-end, high-brow boutiques if what you could conveniently afford is available only at the rummage sales outlets, (what we call *bend-down-boutique, tokunbo, okrika, or bosikona* in Nigeria); you could upgrade when your finances improve; don't buy a car if you can't maintain it.

Please, this is not poverty mentality! Life is in stages; with patience you'll get to the place you desire.

I'd also like to borrow the quote from Warren Buffet, one the richest men in the world!

"*Do not save what is left after spending; but spend what is left after saving*"!

No matter how small, set something aside for investment and for unforeseen events that could occur in the future.

If you do this, you won't be caught unawares by sudden financial needs for which you were not prepared; and you're less likely to be subjected to money-worries!

LESSON #55

MANAGE YOUR CONQUESTS

Nothing creates enemies in the corporate battle-field as much as recognition and reward for ideas successfully executed.

As a new-kid-on-the-block, you become the subject-of-envy, malice and back-biting particularly from some of the existing staff who erroneously believe your ideas should have come from them.

They fail to realize, it's just not enough to have ideas, but successful introduction, execution and completion is the key to recognition and reward.

Given the above scenario, you'd do well to avoid getting on a high horse, with your nose in the air. Such attitude will increase your enemies and it could run contrary to your goal of rapid integration and growth within the system.

Always remember there will forever be people who are ready to shoot down your air craft as it climbs! These ones, rather get to work to do something positive with their hands, would prefer to get down to the *"pull-him-down"* task of picking holes in your work trying to find faults.

Don't waste your time listening to such folks; focus on your vision and keep making progress. While they're busy picking holes, get busy climbing and advancing.

LESSON #56
MAKE YOUR EXIT IN AN ACCEPTABLE MANNER

This is probably one of the most valuable of all because it determines the continuity or otherwise of an amicable relationship between you and your employers.

Don't put on the attitude of "I'm-done-with-you-guys". You may be tempted to think "I'm not likely to have anything to do with this company again". Right? Wrong!

Don't burn the bridge when leaving your employers. You may need that bridge in the future. Always remember that saying: "No man is an island". We would all need each other at one time or the other.

Don't leave your employers without giving adequate notice even if you're leaving on a dis-satisfied note. Always remember it is not easy to run an organisation, as you too are likely to find out if you venture into running a business enterprise on your own.

LESSON #57

APPRECIATE GOD ALWAYS

In closing, I would not like to go into an argument about the existence of God or otherwise.

Every individual's choice of worship is personal and must be respected if we're to have an enduring peaceful co-existence in the world.

Individuals must be allowed the freedom to determine their own mode of worship without condemnation from believers of other faiths.

You must learn to respect each person's mode and choice of worship and belief if you want others to respect yours too!

It is an extension of the "Golden Rule": **Do to others what you would like others do to you!**

Mitchell Zuckoff, author and Journalism professor at Boston University, gave an account of the thoughts and frustrations of Jack Silva, former Navy SEAL, and operative at the Annex in Benghazi, Libya, in the book "**13 Hours** - *The Inside Account of What Really Happened in Benghazi*":

"Everybody has their own idea of whom and what God is. Nobody's right, nobody's wrong. The simple truth is nobody knows, so you have faith.

If you grew up in China, your idea of how things happened and how they are is different than if you grew up in South America or in the Middle East. For someone to say that my way is the right one and everybody else's is wrong or naïve is completely ignorant."

The truth is there is a Supreme Being who oversees and directs affairs of all human beings.

Christians call Him the Almighty God. He is **Yahweh** in Hebrew. He is called **Allah** in the Arabic language.

Yorubas call Him **Olodumare**. Hausas call Him **Ubangiji**. Igbos call Him **Chineke**.

He is God, the **I am that I am.** He is not a man. He is worthy of our praise, worship, and adoration on a daily basis.

We need to learn to live with one another in the true spirit of the love and peace preached by both Christianity and Islam. To my Christian brothers and sisters, I say Shalom; to my Muslim brothers and sisters, I say Salaam Alaikum. May the peace and love of God be with you all.

Whatever your faith or mode of worship, every day, make it a habit to thank, praise, and worship Him that you have the privilege of being an employee in your present workplace.

It could only have been by the mercy, grace, and favour of God, and not by your understanding, wisdom, knowledge, or experience alone.

There must have been divine input, somehow, and somewhere along the way!

In the morning, thank, praise, and worship Him for the new day. Commit your ways to Him;

ask Him to direct and empower you to carry out your activities for the day.

As the day goes by, give Him thanks, praise, and worship for the things He has enabled you to accomplish so far in the course of the day.

At the end of the day, before you sleep, give Him a sacrifice of thanks, praise, and worship for the day as a whole, and for the days ahead.

The Founding Pastor of the Christ Living-Spring Apostolic Mission, Lagos, Nigeria taught us a song of thanksgiving.

Please permit me to share it with you.

Call: *For all that you have done*

Response: *I will sing Halleluyah*

Call: *For all that you are doing*

Response: *I will sing Halleluyah*

Call: *For all that you will do*

Response: *I will sing Halleluyah*

Sing Halleluyah

Unto thee Lord

AFTER-WORD

The common outcomes of lessons learnt in a corporate environment are two-fold; either you apply those lessons as you continue to work and blend into the scene, or you apply them in your own business as an entrepreneur to equip your staff.

Now, whichever option you've decided to choose, you owe it a duty to teach new intakes into the corporate front-line, the lessons you've learnt through this book which reinforce your experience on the job.

On the other hand, you could recommend this book to new employees to fast-track their integration into the organisation, as well as rapid adoption of its culture and values.

Please note that this book is designed to jump-start you into thinking and taking actions that would enhance a smooth integration into the corporate world.

It's not necessarily a one-foot-after-the-other standard or set of rules cast in stone. The lessons could be adapted to suit your peculiar circumstance.

The bottom-line is that, in embarking on a journey, you're most likely to make lesser mistakes if you learn from the mistakes and experience of those who travelled that road before you.

Always remember, *"every cloud has a silver lining"*. You too will pull through and excel in your new work environment. No matter the initial obstacles you may encounter at the early stages of your integration into the system, this book is geared to power you through them!

While you're celebrating your graduation and new J.O.B, you must be conscious of the fact that the workplace is a rough terrain. Get prepared for the challenges that are bound to come.

Good luck.

B.S.A

ACKNOWLEDGEMENT

My sincere thanks go to the members of the Body of Christ at the Chosen Generation Parish of the Redeemed Christian Church of God, as well as my colleagues at Hotel Support Services Limited, Skyway Aviation Handling Company Limited, and SIFAX Nigeria Limited, Lagos, Nigeria. I'm equally grateful to all my neighbours.

You all helped me bring out invaluable gems out of dregs.

I'm particularly grateful to preachers of the gospel for their messages from the pulpit and through the print and electronic media.

I'm grateful to the entire members of the Balogun-Adepetu family. Specifically, to my two brothers, Prof. J.A Adepetu and Mr. J.A Adepetu, who made sure I had a sound education.

Pa Noah Akinola Adepetu, thank you for bridging the gap and

showing me fatherly love when Baba answered the divine call to be with the Lord.

Thanks for your love and care.

I'm also grateful to the lovely women who gracefully left their families and joined the Balogun-Adepetu family – my aunties, wives, and mummies. Lots of love to you all!

Of course, I haven't forgotten my other siblings, their spouses, and especially, my lovely nephews, nieces, and cousins.

You have all been a blessing to me. You have been specially ordained by the Almighty and Omniscient God to play different goal-oriented and motivating roles in my life.

I say you've been more like brothers and sisters to me. Thank you for sharing your views and aspirations with me without any restraint. Thanks for your love. I love you all.

May the Almighty God keep alive amongst us, the fire of His love.

After man was created, the Almighty God, in His infinite wisdom created a woman to be a suitable assistant to him. He said it is not good for the man to be alone. I have not been alone on this project; I've had the support of my friend and wife, to whom I'm grateful for her suggestions.

I'm grateful to friends and colleagues who took out time to go through the manuscript and made useful suggestions.

Thanks to the entire members of the publishers, Create Space (a Division of Amazon, Inc.) for putting this book together in its present format.

Above all, my appreciation goes to the Almighty God, my greatest source of inspiration, for giving me a sound mind, and the grace to start and complete this project.

Other books written by BSA:

Book 1: TWENTY-FOUR SEVEN

This book discusses how to run the race of life successfully under guidance and vision from the Supreme Being, the Almighty God.

Find out from this book how to key in to divine guidance and vision which a lot of us often call a flash of ideas, intuition or "gut-feeling"; that strong feeling to act.

Don't live your life with a "hit-or-miss" attitude. Find out from this book how to:

- Put a plan of action in place and run with it without delay.
- Take time to check out how you're doing on your project, to know whether or not you're achieving your goals in line with your vision.
- Have a positive attitude towards life even when negative words and

distractions come, as they are bound to come from the world.
- Rest from work and give thanks to the Almighty God, the maker of all things and the one who gives life and hope for tomorrow.
- Available at:
- www.amazon.com

Book 2: KINGDOM SEEDLINGS

(Coloured interior)

This book is a collection of poems for children and the young-at-heart.

The poems are presented in terms of everyday experiences, and issues with which children can easily relate.

It makes use of easy-to-understand words. It also provides an explanation of a few not-so-common words and idioms.

It also brings children to understand, obey, love, respect, and to learn to trust God.

This book will teach your child to have a balanced view of life and grow to be a responsible adult.

Available at:
- www.amazon.com

Book 3: KINGDOM SEEDLINGS

(Black-and-White interior)

Available at:
- www.amazon.com

Book 4: PLAYING GAMES WITH THE HI VIRUS

(Black-and-White interior)

This book is a collection of the author's thoughts about the humanity-endangering disease, the HI Virus (HIV), which is generally believed to be the cause of the Acquired Immuno-Deficiency Syndrome, (AIDS).

The poems are presented in terms of everyday experiences, and issues with which the general public can easily relate.

It makes use of easy-to-understand words to bring home the reality of the disease, and the need to take precautions.

It goes beyond playing games and politics. It goes beyond the belief that it is an intention to scare and discourage young people from having intimate sexual relationships before marriage.

Spread the word, not the disease.

Available at:

- www.amazon.com (Black-and-White)

Book 5: PLAYING GAMES WITH THE HI VIRUS

(Coloured interior)

- www.amazon.com
  (Coloured Interior)

Book 6: Oops!

Have you ever been in a situation where you said something you wished you never said?

Spoken words are like broken eggs; difficult to re-assemble!

"OOPS!" is a new book that will show you how to avoid the discomfort and embarrassment of having to take back your words!

Available at:

(**e-Book** Version)

http://bookstore.westbowpress.com/Products/CategoryCenter/REL!019/Counseling.aspx

(**Paper-back** Version)

- www.amazon.com

They are also available for borrowing on Amazon's Kindle Select programme

Book 7: Watch your Words!

Have you ever been in a situation where you said something you wished you never said?

Spoken words are like bullets; once fired, they're difficult to retrieve!

An unkind word is like a bullet. It can kill a man's spirit, soul, and body

You can make someone's heart glad or sad by your words.

"*WATCH YOUR WORDS!*" is a new easy-to-read, quick reference book that will show you how to avoid the discomfort and embarrassment of having to take back your words!

- www.amazon.com

8. After the Wedding Bells
(Black-and-White Interior)

- www.amazon.com

Have you ever wondered how two individuals from different backgrounds could come together, get married, and stay together *"for better, or for worse..."*

In the book **"After the Wedding Bells"**, Samuel reveals lessons you need to know to enable you and your partner stay together in a marriage relationship, such as:

Don't deceive your partner; Learn to say Thank you; Manage your money; Cope with your In-laws; Mentor your children; Learn to apologise; Learn to forgive, and many other LESSONs.

"After the Wedding Bells" is a no-frills, short-and-sharp reference booklet that reveals time-tested secrets couples need to make their marriage last long.

Book 9: After the Wedding Bells
(Coloured Interior)

Available at:

- www.amazon.com

Please visit our blog: www.bsafam.com

Contact:

e-Mail: sammydaniels3@yahoo.com

Mobile: +234-8038261705; +234-8095580812

www.ingramcontent.com/pod-product-compliance
Lightning Source LLC
Chambersburg PA
CBHW020900180526
45163CB00007B/2577